FROM DEVELOPER TO TECH LEAD

ELEVATE YOUR SKILLS, EMPOWER TOUR TEAM, AND SHAPE THE FUTURE

OWEN **FRANSSEN**

Contents

<u>Demystifying Technical Leadership: What It Really Means</u>

Part 1: The Foundations of Technical Leadership

Welcome to the world of tech leadership! If you're here, chances are you're already on the path to becoming a rockstar tech leader. But before you dive headfirst into leading teams, solving problems, and making groundbreaking decisions, it's crucial to lay a solid foundation of essential skills, knowledge, and the right mindset.

This first section is your guide to building that foundation. We'll explore the fundamental principles of effective leadership, empowering you to navigate complex challenges, assemble high-performing teams, and foster a culture of innovation and continuous improvement. Whether you're an aspiring tech leader or a seasoned professional seeking to refine your leadership skills, this section will equip you with the tools and insights to impact the ever-changing tech landscape significantly.

The Road to Becoming a Tech Boss

Welcome to the exciting world of technical leadership, where you get to combine your passion for technology with your knack for inspiring and guiding others. In this first chapter, we'll explore the path to becoming an exceptional tech leader, a journey filled with challenges, growth, and the satisfaction of shaping the future of technology.

First, let's clear up a common misconception: becoming a tech leader isn't just about being a technical expert. Sure, having strong technical skills is essential, but it's just one piece of the puzzle..

Technical leadership is about understanding the human side of technology. It's about leading teams of talented individuals, fostering innovation, and navigating the ever-changing technological landscape.

Tech leaders are the ones who turn ideas into reality, who empower their teams to push boundaries, and who inspire others to embrace the power of technology. They're the visionaries who see the potential of technology to transform industries, improve lives, and make a real difference in the world.

What Makes a Technical Leader Different?

Technical leaders possess a unique blend of skills and qualities that set them apart. They're not just tech experts; they're also effective communicators, problem solvers, and decision-makers. They have the ability to see the big picture, to connect the dots between technology and business goals, and to translate complex technical concepts into understandable language.

But above all, tech leaders are passionate about technology. They're driven by curiosity and a desire to learn. They're the ones who stay up late reading about new trends, who experiment with emerging technologies, and who are constantly seeking ways to apply technology to solve real-world problems.

The Path to Technical Leadership

The path to technical leadership is not a one-size-fits-all journey. There are many different routes to the top, and the best path for you will depend on your unique skills, experiences, and aspirations.

Some tech leaders start their careers as engineers or programmers, working their way up the ranks through their technical expertise and leadership potential. Others may come from a business or management background, bringing their understanding of organizational dynamics and strategic planning to the table.

Regardless of your background, there are certain core skills and qualities that are essential for success as a technical leader. These include:

Technical expertise: A deep understanding of the technologies you're working with is crucial. You need to be able to grasp complex technical concepts and translate them into understandable language for your team and stakeholders.

Communication skills: Effective communication is essential for leading a team and building relationships. You need to be able to articulate your vision, provide clear instructions, and foster open and honest communication within your team.

Problem-solving skills: The ability to identify problems, analyze them from different angles, and develop creative solutions is critical for technical leadership. You'll constantly face challenges and setbacks, and your ability to think outside the box and find solutions will be key to your success.

Decision-making skills: As a tech leader, you'll be making decisions that have a significant impact on your team and organization. You need to be able to weigh different options, consider risks and potential consequences, and make sound decisions under pressure.

Leadership skills: Technical leadership is about more than just technical expertise; it's about inspiring and motivating others. You need to be able to build trust, empower your team, and create a culture of innovation and collaboration.

Your Next Steps

The first step on your journey to technical leadership is to develop a deep understanding of the technologies you're working with. Stay up-to-date on the latest trends, experiment with new tools and techniques, and never stop learning.

As you gain technical expertise, start to develop your leadership skills. Take on more responsibility within your team, volunteer for projects that require leadership, and seek out opportunities to mentor and coach others.

And remember, the path to technical leadership is not a linear one. There will be setbacks, challenges, and moments of self-doubt along the way. But with perseverance, a willingness to learn, and a passion for technology, you have the potential to become an exceptional tech leader who makes a real impact on the world.

Demystifying Technical Leadership: What It Really Means

Technical leadership often gets painted as a mythical creature, shrouded in mystery and only accessible to a select few. But in reality, technical leadership is not about possessing superhuman abilities or having a secret decoder ring; it's about understanding the unique combination of skills, qualities, and mindsets that make an exceptional tech leader.

The Technical Leader's Toolkit

Technical leaders are not just tech experts; they're a blend of strategist, motivator, and problem solver. They possess a unique toolkit that allows them to navigate the complexities of the tech world while inspiring and guiding their teams towards success.

A solid foundation in technology is essential. Understanding the intricacies of the technologies you're working with allows you to make informed decisions, communicate effectively, and troubleshoot problems efficiently.

Technical leaders are not just experts in their field; they're also masters of communication. as a tech lead you should be able to translate complex technical concepts into understandable language, bridge the gap between technical and non-technical stakeholders, and create a culture of open and honest dialogue within your team.

The tech world is constantly evolving, throwing new challenges and opportunities our way. Technical leaders thrive in this dynamic environment, approaching problems with a methodical and analytical mindset, seeking creative solutions, and adapting to ever-changing circumstances.

Don't be afraid to make decisions, even when faced with uncertainty. Gather information, weigh options, consider risks and potential consequences, and make sound judgments that guides your team forward.

Technical leaders inspire and motivate others, creating a positive and productive work environment. They foster trust, empower their team members to take ownership, and cultivate a culture of innovation and collaboration.

The Technical Leader's Mindset

Technical leadership is not just about the skills and qualities you possess; it's also about the mindset you bring to the table. Technical leaders approach their work with a growth mindset, embracing challenges as opportunities to learn and improve.

Technical leaders are never satisfied with the status quo. As an aspiring lead, you should constantly seek new knowledge, explore emerging technologies, and expand your skillset to stay ahead of the curve.

As a lead you need to understand that feedback is a gift, not a criticism. Actively seek feedback from colleagues, mentors, and stakeholders, then use it to identify areas for growth and refine your leadership approach.

Technical leaders are comfortable with change and uncertainty. You should embrace new technologies, adapt to evolving market trends, and pivot strategies when necessary to ensure your team remains competitive and successful.

You should have the ability to recognize your limitations and be open to learning from others. As you approach situations with humility, acknowledge your strengths and weaknesses, and seek guidance when needed.

As a technical leader, you are genuinely passionate about technology. You see its potential to transform industries, improve lives, and make a real difference in the world. This passion will fuel your drive, creativity, and commitment to innovation.

Becoming an Exceptional Technical Leader

Technical leadership is not a destination but a continuous journey of learning, growth, and development. By cultivating the skills, qualities, and mindset described above, you can become an exceptional technical leader who inspires, motivates, and guides your team towards achieving remarkable results.

Remember, technical leadership is not about being perfect or having all the answers; it's about embracing the challenges, learning from your mistakes, and continuously striving to improve. With dedication, perseverance, and a genuine passion for technology, you have the potential to make a lasting impact as an exceptional technical leader.

Characteristics of Effective Technical Leaders

In the tech world, where change is the only constant, effective technical leaders stand out like beacons of light, guiding their teams through the maze of innovation and inspiration. They're not just tech whizzes; they're problem solvers, motivators, and strategists who possess a unique blend of skills that make them truly extraordinary.

The Secrets to Effective Technical Leadership

Effective technical leaders aren't simply born with their skills; they're crafted through a combination of natural talent, hard work, and a genuine passion for technology. Some of the essential qualities that make them so effective include:

Being tech-savvy: A solid understanding of the technologies you work with is a must-have as a technical leader. You need to be able to grasp complex technical concepts, explain them in a way that everyone can understand, and stay up-to-date on the latest trends.

Have problem-solving prowess: The tech world is full of challenges, and technical leaders are the ones who tackle them head-on. You should be able to analyze problems from multiple angles, think creatively, and come up with solutions that work.

Be a communication chameleon: In the position of a technical leader, you should be able to talk tech to the techies and translate it into plain English for the non-techies. You need the ability to communicate effectively with all levels of your team and stakeholders, ensuring that everyone is on the same page.

Have leadership mojo: You need to inspire and motivate your team to achieve great things and create a positive and supportive work environment where everyone feels appreciated and valued.

Have strategic vision: Technical leaders don't just focus on the here and now. You need to always be looking ahead and see how technology can be used to achieve your organization's goals.

Be adaptable and agile: The tech landscape is constantly changing, and you need to be able to roll with the punches. Be comfortable with change and always open to new ideas.

Have decision-making dexterity: As a technical leader, you will often be required to make tough decisions under pressure. You need the ability to weigh all of the options, consider the risks, and make the best decision for the team and the organization.

Be genuinely passionate about technology and its potential to change the world. This passion is contagious and will inspire your team to be just as passionate.

The Impact of Effective Leaders

Technical leaders who embody these essential characteristics have a profound impact on their teams, organizations, and the broader technological landscape. As a lead you will drive innovation, empower individuals, and shape the future of technology. Your leadership will create a ripple effect, driving progress, generating value, and transforming the way your team works.

The Journey to Technical Leadership

The path to technical leadership is not a linear progression; it is a continuous process of learning, growth, and self-discovery. It is not merely about acquiring technical skills; it is about developing the leadership qualities and strategic thinking that enable you to guide teams and organizations towards success. As you embark on this journey, embrace the challenges, celebrate the successes, and never lose sight of your passion for technology and your commitment to making a positive impact through your leadership.

Embrace Continuous Learning

The technological landscape is ever-evolving, and effective technical leaders must remain at the forefront of these advancements. Dedicate yourself to continuous learning, exploring new technologies, and expanding your knowledge base. Attend industry conferences, participate in online courses, and engage with fellow professionals to stay ahead of the curve.

Connect with experienced technical leaders who can provide mentorship and guidance as you navigate your career path. Their insights and experiences can prove invaluable in shaping your leadership skills and perspectives. Seek opportunities to shadow experienced leaders, ask questions, and learn from their successes and challenges.

Effective communication is a cornerstone of technical leadership. Practice articulating complex technical concepts in a clear and concise manner, tailoring your communication style to your audience. Hone your presentation skills, engage in active listening, and strive to create a dialogue that fosters understanding and collaboration.

Volunteer for leadership roles within your team or organization. These opportunities provide valuable experience in motivating, guiding, and empowering others to achieve common goals. Step outside your comfort zone, embrace challenges, and learn from your experiences as a leader.

Regularly seek feedback from colleagues, mentors, and supervisors. Use this feedback to identify areas for improvement and refine your leadership skills. Engage in self-reflection, evaluating your strengths, weaknesses, and areas for growth. Continuous self-improvement is crucial for effective technical leadership.

Cultivate a network of professional connections within the technology industry. Engage with peers, attend industry events, and participate in online forums. Building a strong network provides access to valuable insights, opportunities, and support.

The journey to technical leadership is not without its challenges and setbacks. View these as opportunities for growth and learning. Resilience, perseverance, and a positive attitude are essential for navigating these challenges and emerging stronger.

Acknowledge and celebrate your accomplishments along the way. Recognize the contributions of your team members and celebrate collective successes. Taking time to appreciate your progress and achievements will fuel your motivation and drive.

While dedication and passion for your work are important, maintaining a healthy work-life balance is crucial for long-term success. Prioritize your well-being, engage in activities you enjoy, and nurture your personal life. A healthy mind and body will enhance your leadership effectiveness.

The journey to technical leadership is an ongoing process of learning, growth, and adaptation. Embrace lifelong learning, stay curious about new technologies, and continuously seek opportunities to expand your knowledge and skillset.

Remember, the path to technical leadership is not about reaching a destination but about embarking on a continuous journey of transformation and growth. Embrace the challenges, celebrate the successes, and never lose sight of the profound impact you can have on the world through your leadership. As you navigate this journey, you will not only become an effective technical leader but also a lifelong learner, a catalyst for innovation, and an inspiration to others.

Part 2: Mastering the Technical Landscape

In the tech world, where innovation is the name of the game, technical leaders need to be on top of their stuff. They've got to understand the latest trends, master the cutting-edge technologies, and navigate the ever-changing landscape with confidence.

This section is your go-to guide for staying ahead of the curve and becoming a true expert in your field. We'll break down the intricacies of the tech industry, giving you the knowledge and strategies you need to make informed decisions, guide your team through complex challenges, and position yourself as a leader who knows their stuff.

Whether you're venturing into uncharted tech territories or deepening your expertise in your chosen field, this section will equip you with the skills and confidence to lead your team into the future of tech. So, grab your laptop, put on your thinking cap, and get ready to embark on a journey to becoming a technical leader who's always one step ahead.

Staying Ahead of the Curve: Embracing Continuous Learning

The ability to stay ahead of the curve is not just an advantage; it is a necessity for effective technical leadership. As technology continues to transform industries, reshape our lives, and redefine the boundaries of what is possible, technical leaders must embrace continuous learning as a fundamental principle of their leadership approach.

In the past, technical expertise was often seen as a static set of skills that could be acquired through formal education and experience. However, the rapid pace of technological advancements has rendered this traditional view obsolete. Today, as an effective technical leader you must be a lifelong learner, constantly expanding your knowledge base, adapting to new trends, and mastering emerging technologies.

The reasons for this imperative are clear:

Technology is disrupting industries at an unprecedented pace, rendering traditional skills and knowledge obsolete. As a technical leader, you must stay ahead of these disruptions to ensure that your organization remains relevant, competitive, and innovative.

The skillsets required for success in technology are constantly evolving. New programming languages, frameworks, and tools emerge regularly, demanding that you remain up-to-date to effectively guide your team.

Effective technical leaders must make informed decisions that align with the organization's overall strategic goals. Continuous learning ensures you have a comprehensive understanding of emerging trends and their potential impact.

Technical leaders must empower their teams to adapt and thrive in the ever-changing technological landscape. By demonstrating a commitment to continuous learning, you set the example and encourage your team to embrace lifelong learning as well.

Strategies for Embracing Continuous Learning

Embracing continuous learning as a technical leader requires a proactive and systematic approach.

Set clear learning goals for yourself, identifying specific technologies, skills, or areas of expertise you want to develop. Create a structured learning plan that outlines the resources, methods, and timeframe for achieving your goals.

Utilize a variety of learning methods to cater to your preferences and learning styles. Attend industry conferences, participate in online courses, read industry publications, engage in hands-on coding projects, and seek mentorship from experienced professionals.

Build a network of colleagues, mentors, and experts in your field. Engage in discussions, attend industry meetups, and participate in online forums to gain insights into emerging trends and perspectives from experienced professionals.

Participating in open-source projects can provide hands-on experience with new technologies, collaboration opportunities, and exposure to diverse approaches to problem-solving.

Never Stop Learning. Make continuous learning a way of life. Cultivate a growth mindset, embrace challenges as opportunities for growth, and never lose your curiosity and passion for exploring new knowledge.

The Rewards of Continuous Learning

The benefits of continuous learning extend far beyond staying ahead of the curve. By embracing a lifelong learning approach, you will reap numerous rewards.

Continuous learning deepens your understanding of technologies, enabling you to make informed decisions, guide your teams effectively, and contribute to groundbreaking innovations.

As your technical knowledge expands, so does your strategic value to the organization. You can identify opportunities, assess risks, and guide the organization towards innovative solutions.

Your commitment to continuous learning sets an example for your team, fostering a culture of lifelong learning, innovation, and adaptability.

The process of continuous learning is intrinsically rewarding, providing a sense of personal growth, fulfillment, and satisfaction.

As your technical expertise and leadership skills grow, you open doors to new career opportunities and advancements.

Staying ahead of the curve in the ever-evolving world of technology is not a sprint but a marathon. By embracing continuous learning as a fundamental principle of your leadership approach, you not only enhance your technical expertise and strategic value but also empower your teams and drive innovation.

Deepening Your Technical Expertise

Deepening your technical expertise is a cornerstone of effective technical leadership. It is the foundation upon which you build your ability to make informed decisions, guide your team effectively, and contribute to groundbreaking innovations. In the ever-evolving world of technology, technical leaders must continuously expand their knowledge base and stay abreast of emerging trends to remain at the forefront of their field.

The Significance of Technical Expertise

Technical expertise is not just about possessing a vast array of technical facts and figures; it is about understanding the underlying principles, concepts, and frameworks that drive technological advancements.

Technical leaders must be able to analyze complex technical problems, assess potential solutions, and make informed decisions that align with the organization's overall goals. Deep technical expertise will set the foundation for sound decision-making.

Technical leaders are responsible for guiding and mentoring their teams, ensuring that they have the skills and knowledge to tackle complex technical challenges. Deep technical expertise will allow you to provide effective guidance, identify areas for improvement, and help team members reach their full potential.

Technical leaders play a pivotal role in driving innovation within their organizations. Deep technical expertise will enable you to identify new opportunities, explore emerging technologies, and contribute to the development of groundbreaking solutions.

Strategies for Deepening Technical Expertise

Deepening your technical expertise requires a proactive and focused approach.

Ensure you have a strong grasp of the fundamental principles of computer science, programming languages, and relevant technologies. This solid foundation will enable you to learn new technologies more effectively and adapt to changing landscapes.

Prioritize learning technologies that align with your current role and career aspirations. Research industry trends, identify emerging technologies, and focus on acquiring expertise in areas that will enhance your value and contribution.

Engage in hands-on coding exercises, participate in hackathons, and build personal projects. Practical application of your knowledge will solidify your understanding and enhance your problem-solving skills.

Keep abreast of industry standards, best practices, and emerging frameworks. This ensures that your technical knowledge remains relevant and aligned with current industry expectations.

Make continuous learning a habit. Attend industry conferences, participate in online courses, read industry publications, and explore new technologies regularly.

The Benefits of Deepening Technical Expertise

The benefits of deepening your technical expertise extend far beyond simply being able to solve complex technical problems. It enhances your leadership capabilities, expands your career opportunities, and contributes to your overall professional growth and success.

Deep technical expertise establishes you as a credible leader in your field, gaining the respect and trust of your team members and colleagues.

As your technical expertise deepens, so does your ability to identify root causes, devise creative solutions, and tackle complex technical challenges effectively.

Deep technical knowledge enables you to communicate technical concepts clearly and concisely, bridging the gap between technical and non-technical audiences.

Technical expertise provides a foundation for strategic thinking, enabling you to make informed decisions that align with the organization's long-term goals.

Deep technical expertise opens doors to new career opportunities, promotions, and leadership positions within the technology industry.

Deepening your technical expertise is an ongoing journey of learning, exploration, and refinement. It is a commitment to staying ahead of the curve, expanding your knowledge base, and mastering the ever-evolving technological landscape. By cultivating technical expertise, you become a more effective technical leader, empowering your teams, driving innovation, and shaping the future of technology. Embrace the challenges, celebrate the successes, and never lose your passion for learning and growth as you navigate this rewarding journey of technical leadership.

Cultivating a Growth Mindset

In the dynamic and ever-evolving world of technology, a growth mindset is not just a desirable trait; it is an essential ingredient for effective technical leadership. A growth mindset is the belief that your abilities can be developed through dedication and hard work, rather than being fixed at birth. This mindset fosters a willingness to learn, embrace challenges, and continuously improve.

Technical leaders must navigate a constantly changing landscape, adapt to new trends, and guide their teams towards innovation. A growth mindset will empower you to embrace these challenges with a positive attitude and a belief in your ability to learn and grow.

With a growth mindset you will view setbacks and challenges as opportunities for learning and growth. You won't be easily discouraged by failures, but rather use them as motivation to refine your skills and strategies.

A growth mindset engenders a commitment to lifelong learning. Actively seek out new knowledge, explore different technologies, and embrace opportunities to expand your skillset.

A growth mindset extends beyond yourself. Set an example for your teams, encouraging them to embrace challenges, learn from mistakes, and continuously improve their skills. This creates a culture of innovation and adaptability within the organization.

A growth mindset will help you to approach problems from multiple angles, seek diverse perspectives, and no bet afraid to experiment with new ideas. This openness to new approaches fosters creativity and innovation.

With a growth mindset, you will be able to assess emerging trends, identify opportunities, and adapt your strategies to align with the ever-changing technological landscape.

Strategies for Cultivating a Growth Mindset

Developing a growth mindset is not a sudden transformation; it is an ongoing process that requires conscious effort and dedication.

View challenges and setbacks as opportunities for growth and learning. Analyze what went wrong, identify areas for improvement, and use these experiences to refine your skills and strategies.

Recognize and celebrate your accomplishments along the way. Taking time to appreciate your progress will reinforce your growth mindset and motivate you to continue learning and improving.

Actively seek feedback from mentors, colleagues, and supervisors. Use this feedback to identify areas for improvement and refine your skills and leadership approach.

Step outside your comfort zone and embrace new experiences and opportunities. This will broaden your perspectives, expand your knowledge base, and enhance your adaptability.

Maintain a lifelong commitment to learning. Embrace new technologies, explore different areas of expertise, and never lose your curiosity and passion for learning.

The Impact of a Growth Mindset on Technical Leadership

The impact of a growth mindset on technical leadership is profound and far-reaching. It empowers technical leaders to:

- Navigate the ever-changing technological landscape with confidence and adaptability.
- Foster a culture of continuous learning, innovation, and resilience within their teams.
- Guide their teams towards groundbreaking advancements and shape the future of technology.

Cultivating a growth mindset is an essential step in becoming an effective technical leader. It is the foundation upon which you can build your technical expertise, strategic vision, and ability to empower and inspire your teams. Embrace the challenges, celebrate the successes, and never lose sight of the transformative power of technology and your role in shaping its future.

Becoming a Tech Trend Spotter

Effective technical leaders must possess deep technical expertise, strategic thinking and the ability to identify emerging trends and assess their potential impact. Tech trend spotting is a crucial skill for technical leaders, enabling them to stay ahead of the curve, make informed decisions, and guide their organisations towards innovation and success.

The Importance of Tech Trend Spotting for Technical Leaders

Technical leaders play a pivotal role in shaping the future of technology. By identifying emerging trends, you will be able to:

Anticipate Technological Disruptions: Tech trend spotters can recognize the potential impact of emerging technologies and prepare their organizations to adapt and thrive in the face of disruption.

Inform Strategic Decision-Making: Identifying trends provides you with valuable insights to inform strategic decisions about resource allocation, product development, and market positioning.

Drive Innovation: Tech trend spotters can identify opportunities to leverage emerging technologies to develop innovative solutions, products, and services.

Empower Teams and Foster Agility: By keeping your team abreast of emerging trends, you empower them to adapt, innovate, and remain at the forefront of their respective fields.

Strategies for Becoming a Tech Trend Spotter

Effective tech trend spotting requires a combination of curiosity, observation, and critical thinking.

Approach the world with an open mind and a constant curiosity about new technologies, emerging trends, and societal shifts.

Read industry publications, follow thought leaders, and engage with experts from various fields to gain a holistic understanding of technological advancements.

Pay attention to how people interact with technology, identify emerging consumer preferences, and monitor market shifts to identify potential trends.

Understand the underlying factors driving technological advancements, such as demographic changes, economic trends, and societal shifts. This understanding will help you to identify potential disruptive innovations.

Actively participate in online forums, attend industry conferences, and engage with fellow tech enthusiasts to stay informed about emerging trends and connect with potential collaborators.

Dedicate time to experiment with new technologies, attend workshops, and participate in hackathons to gain hands-on experience and identify potential applications.

Create a framework to assess the potential impact of emerging trends. Consider factors such as feasibility, market viability, and potential benefits and risks.

Continuously share your insights and observations with colleagues, mentors, and the broader tech community. Collaboration can foster new ideas and enhance your trend spotting abilities.

The Rewards of Tech Trend Spotting

Becoming a tech trend spotter has numerous rewards that extend beyond professional recognition and career advancement.

By identifying and promoting promising trends, you play a direct role in shaping the future of technology and its impact on your organization.

Your ability to anticipate trends positions your organization to adapt, innovate, and thrive in the ever-changing technological landscape.

Your insights and expertise make you a valuable resource for your organization, enabling you to provide guidance and make informed decisions.

The continuous learning, exploration, and problem-solving involved in tech trend spotting provide immense personal satisfaction and growth.

Tech trend spotting is not just a skill; it is a mindset that empowers technical leaders to navigate the complexities of the technological landscape, anticipate disruptive innovations, and guide their organizations towards success. By embracing this mindset and cultivating the strategies outlined in this chapter, you can become a tech trend spotter, a catalyst for innovation, and a leader who shapes the future of technology.

Part 3: Honing Your Leadership Skills

This section is all about taking your technical expertise to the next level and transforming you into an exceptional tech leader. We'll dive into the essential leadership skills you need to inspire, motivate, and guide your team towards achieving remarkable results.

Get ready to master effective communication, team building, conflict resolution, and decision-making. These skills will not only enhance your ability to lead and manage your team effectively but also transform you into a respected and influential figure within your organization and the broader tech community.

Whether you're an aspiring tech leader or a seasoned pro seeking to polish your leadership skills, this section is packed with practical tips and insights that will elevate your leadership game to new heights. Grab a cup of coffee, put on your thinking cap, and let's embark on this journey to becoming an exceptional tech leader!

Communication: The Bridge Between Technology and People

In an ever-evolving landscape, effective communication is the cornerstone of successful technical leadership. It is the bridge that connects the complexities of technology with the needs, aspirations, and understanding of the people who shape and utilize it. Technical leaders who master the art of communication can inspire, motivate, and empower their teams to achieve groundbreaking advancements, while those who struggle to communicate effectively risk creating misunderstandings, fostering resistance to change, and hindering innovation.

The Significance of Communication for Technical Leaders

Communication is not just about exchanging information; it is about building connections, fostering understanding, and aligning diverse perspectives towards a common goal. To be an effective technical leader you need to recognize that communication is a two-way street, requiring not only the ability to articulate complex ideas clearly but also the skill to listen actively and empathize with different viewpoints.

As a technical lead you must bridge the gap between the technical and non-technical worlds, translating complex technological concepts into language that is accessible and understandable to all stakeholders.

Effective communication is the foundation for collaboration and innovation. It will enable you to share ideas, gather feedback, and harness the collective expertise of your team to solve complex problems and develop groundbreaking solutions.

Technological advancements often require behavioral changes and organizational adaptations. Effective communication is essential for guiding teams through these changes, addressing concerns, and promoting change thus fostering a culture of acceptance and adoption.

Clear, consistent, and transparent communication also helps to build trust and credibility among team members, stakeholders, and the broader organization. This trust is essential for effective leadership and achieving shared goals.

As a technical leader who excels at communication you can inspire and empower your team, igniting passion, motivating individuals to contribute their best, and fostering a sense of shared purpose and ownership.

Strategies for Mastering Effective Technical Communication

Effective technical communication requires a blend of skills, knowledge, and conscious effort. Following are some strategies to enhance your communication effectiveness as a technical leader.

Know your audience. Tailor your communication style and terminology to the audience you are addressing. Consider their level of technical expertise, background, and interests.

Strive for clarity and conciseness in your communication. Avoid jargon and overly technical language, instead using simple, direct language that conveys your message effectively.

Effective communication is a two-way process. Practice active listening, giving your full attention to what others are saying, asking clarifying questions where appropriate, and demonstrating a genuine interest in their perspectives.

Use storytelling and analogies to illustrate complex concepts, making them relatable and engaging for non-technical audiences.

Utilize visual aids, diagrams, and demonstrations to enhance your explanations and provide a visual representation of complex ideas.

Seek feedback from colleagues, mentors, and stakeholders on your communication style and effectiveness. Use this feedback to identify areas for improvement and refine your communication approach.

The Impact of Effective Technical Communication

Effective technical communication has a profound impact on individuals, teams, and organizations.

Your clear and effective communication empowers individuals to understand their roles, contribute their expertise, and feel valued as part of the team.

Effective communication fosters alignment within your team, ensuring that everyone is working towards common goals and objectives.

By bridging the gap between technology and people, effective communication fuels innovation, enabling your team to develop solutions that meet the needs of users and drive organizational success.

Being an effective communicator enhances your reputation and credibility as a technical lead, establishing you as a trusted advisor and thought leader.

Effective communication contributes to a positive and supportive organizational culture, fostering trust, collaboration, and a sense of shared purpose.

Communication is not just a skill; it is a powerful tool that enables technical leaders to connect with people, inspire innovation, and shape the future of technology. By mastering the art of effective communication, you can become a catalyst for change, empowering your team to thrive. Remember, communication is the bridge that connects the complexities of technology with the hearts and minds of the people who bring it to life. Embrace the power of communication, and you will become a leader who not only guides but also inspires and empowers.

Empowering Teams: The Art of Motivation and Guidance

At the heart of effective technical leadership lies the ability to empower and inspire teams to achieve extraordinary results. As a tech lead, you are not just a manager or supervisor; you are a catalyst for innovation, a motivator of excellence, and a guide who helps your team navigate the complexities of the technological landscape. Empowering teams is not about micromanaging or wielding authority but about creating an environment where individuals feel valued, challenged, and supported in reaching their full potential.

Empowering teams is a multifaceted concept that encompasses creating a culture of trust, providing opportunities for growth, and fostering a sense of ownership and shared responsibility. It is about recognizing the unique talents and contributions of each of your team's members, harnessing their collective expertise, and aligning their efforts towards common goals.

Key Principles of Empowering Teams

Effective technical leaders adhere to certain key principles when empowering their teams.

Build a foundation of trust by being open, transparent, and honest with your team members. Share information freely, encourage open communication, and create a psychologically safe environment where team members feel comfortable expressing their ideas and concerns.

Delegate tasks and responsibilities to team members. Provide them with the autonomy to make decisions and take ownership of their work. This fosters a sense of empowerment and encourages individuals to take ownership of their contributions.

Celebrate successes, acknowledge contributions, and provide meaningful recognition for achievements. This reinforces positive behaviours, motivates individuals, and instils a sense of value and appreciation within the team.

Provide regular feedback, both positive and constructive, to help team members identify areas for improvement and refine their skills. Foster a culture of continuous learning and growth where feedback is seen as an opportunity for development rather than criticism.

Offer guidance, mentorship, and support to team members as they navigate challenges and pursue their professional growth. This empowers individuals to develop their skills, overcome obstacles, and reach their full potential.

Foster a culture of collaboration, encouraging team members to share ideas, work together, and leverage their collective expertise. This fosters innovation, problem-solving, and a sense of shared responsibility for the team's success.

The Impact of Empowered Teams

Empowered teams reap numerous benefits, both for individuals and the organization as a whole.

Empowered individuals feel more motivated, engaged, and invested in their work. They take ownership of their contributions, strive for excellence, and take pride in their achievements.

A culture of empowerment encourages creativity, innovation, and out-of-the-box thinking. Team members feel empowered to share ideas, challenge assumptions, and contribute to innovative solutions.

By delegating and empowering your team members, you as a leader will benefit from the collective intelligence and expertise of your team. This leads to more informed decisions that consider diverse perspectives and insights.

Empowered individuals feel valued, and respected. They have a sense of ownership over their work. This leads to increased job satisfaction, reduced turnover, and a more stable and experienced team.

Empowered teams are more productive, innovative, and resilient, contributing significantly to the organization's success and competitive advantage in the ever-evolving technological landscape.

Technical leaders who master the art of empowering their teams unleash a powerful force for innovation, growth, and organizational success. By creating an environment of trust, autonomy, and shared responsibility, you can enable individuals to thrive, teams to excel, and organizations to achieve remarkable results. Remember, effective technical leadership is not just about mastering technology; it is about empowering the human potential within your team to shape the future of technology and make a lasting impact on your organisation.

Navigating Conflict: Fostering a Collaborative Environment

In any team setting, conflict is inevitable. It arises from differences in perspectives, opinions, and approaches to problem-solving. In the dynamic and sometimes high-pressure environment of technical teams, conflict can be particularly challenging to navigate. However, technical leaders who effectively manage conflict can transform it into a catalyst for growth, innovation, and improved team performance.

The Importance of Conflict Management for Technical Leaders

Conflict management is an essential skill for technical leaders, as it enables you to minimise the negative impacts of conflict, such as reduced productivity, strained relationships, and a diminished sense of team cohesion.

As you facilitate constructive dialogue around conflict you create an environment where team members can openly express their concerns, address differences, and find common ground.

Conflict can spark creativity and lead to innovative ideas. It challenges your team members to step outside their comfort zones and consider different perspectives. This clash of ideas is like a brainstorming session on steroids, leading to groundbreaking solutions.

By addressing conflict constructively, you can strengthen relationships within your team, fostering trust and mutual respect.

Effective conflict management contributes to a collaborative culture where team members feel comfortable sharing ideas, taking risks, and working together towards common goals.

Strategies for Navigating Conflict in Technical Teams

Navigating conflict in technical teams is like navigating a tricky obstacle course – it requires finesse, agility, and a touch of empathy. But just like mastering an obstacle course, with the right strategies, you can emerge victorious, your team stronger and more united.

First, nip conflicts in the bud. Don't let them fester and grow into nasty weeds. Address them early, when they're still manageable shoots.

Next, lend an ear that actively listens. Understand each party's perspective, their feelings, and the motivations driving their actions. Be the translator who bridges the gap between their words and their unspoken needs.

Create a safe space where everyone feels comfortable expressing their views. Let them know that their opinions are valued, their feelings are heard, and their perspectives are respected.

Shift the focus from positions to interests. Instead of sticking to their guns, encourage team members to explore the underlying interests and concerns that fuel their positions. This opens up a world of possibilities for compromise and understanding.

Seek common ground, that fertile soil where solutions can grow. Identify areas of agreement, shared goals, and mutual respect. This shared foundation will anchor the team as they navigate towards a resolution.

Encourage creative brainstorming sessions, where everyone is invited to contribute their ideas. Let imagination run wild, and don't be afraid to explore unconventional solutions. Remember, sometimes the most innovative ideas come from the most surprising places.

Once a resolution is reached, clearly document the agreed-upon actions and expectations. This roadmap will prevent future misunderstandings and keep everyone on the same page, marching towards a common goal.

The Benefits of Effective Conflict Management

Effective conflict management in technical teams is like a superpower, transforming tension into teamwork, disagreements into innovation, and challenges into opportunities.

When conflicts are resolved, the tension that once weighed on the team evaporates, replaced by a renewed sense of focus and collaboration. Communication flows freely, ideas are exchanged without fear, and teamwork becomes a well-oiled machine, fueling enhanced team performance.

Conflict, when embraced as a catalyst for growth, ignites a spark of innovation that illuminates the path towards groundbreaking solutions. By encouraging open dialogue, respecting diverse perspectives, and challenging assumptions, teams tap into a reservoir of creativity that would otherwise remain dormant.

Constructively resolving conflicts isn't just about finding solutions; it's about forging stronger relationships within the team. As team members navigate disagreements with empathy, trust blossoms, mutual respect deepens, and a sense of camaraderie takes root.

Teams that can effectively manage conflict are like resilient warriors, poised to adapt and thrive in the face of adversity. They've learned to harness conflict as a tool for growth, emerging from challenges stronger, more adaptable, and ready to conquer new frontiers.

A culture of constructive conflict resolution isn't just a perk; it's a beacon that attracts and retains top talent. Employees seek environments where their voices are heard, their concerns are addressed, and their growth is nurtured. Such a culture fosters a positive and supportive work environment, where individuals feel valued and empowered to contribute their best.

Conflict in technical teams is not a sign of weakness or failure; it is an inevitable and often valuable aspect of the teamwork process.

Technical leaders who can effectively navigate conflict transform it into an opportunity for growth, innovation, and improved team performance. By fostering a culture of open communication, empathy, and constructive dialogue, you can harness the power of conflict to strengthen your team and drive innovation.

Decision-Making: The Weight of Responsibility

As a technical leader, you will face a constant barrage of decisions, each carrying significant weight and potential consequences. Effective decision-making is not just about making the right choice; it is about understanding the complexities of the situation, considering the impact on various stakeholders, and making informed judgments that align with the organization's overall goals and strategic objectives.

The Significance of Effective Decision-Making for Technical Leaders

You play a pivotal role in shaping the success of your team and organization through your decision-making capabilities, making effective decision-making crucial for technical leadership.

As a tech lead the decisions you make guide the development and implementation of technological solutions. Your decisions must align with the organization's strategic direction, ensuring that technology is used to achieve organizational goals and gain a competitive edge.

You must effectively allocate resources, prioritize projects, and make decisions about the timing and scope of technological advancements. These decisions impact the overall efficiency and productivity of your team and the organization as a whole.

Technical leaders must assess risks associated with emerging technologies, potential failures, and changing market conditions. Your decisions will influence the organization's risk profile and ability to navigate challenges and seize opportunities.

Technical leaders are problem solvers. As you face complex technical challenges, your decision-making skills will play a critical role in identifying root causes, developing effective solutions, and fostering a culture of innovation.

The decisions you make as a technical leader have a direct impact on your team's morale and motivation. Informed, well-communicated decisions create a sense of confidence and trust within the team, while poor decisions can lead to frustration, disengagement, and a decline in performance.

Strategies for Enhancing Decision-Making Skills

Effective decision-making is a skill that can be honed and refined through practice and continuous learning. Here are some strategies to enhance your decision-making skills as a technical leader:

Collect comprehensive data, analyze relevant information, and assess the potential impact of each decision option.

Seek input from team members, stakeholders, and experts to gain diverse perspectives and broaden your understanding of the situation.

Carefully weigh the potential risks and benefits of each decision option, considering both short-term and long-term implications.

Ensure that your decisions align with the organization's overall strategic goals, considering the impact on the organization's competitive advantage and future direction.

Clearly communicate your decisions to team members, stakeholders, and affected parties, providing rationale and addressing potential concerns.

Reflect on past decisions. Identify areas for improvement, and incorporate the lessons learned into your future decision-making processes.

Seek guidance from experienced technical leaders and mentors to gain insights, refine your approach, and develop a more strategic decision-making framework.

The Impact of Effective Decision-Making on Technical Leadership

Effective decision-making has a profound impact on the success of technical leaders and the organizations they serve.

Informed decisions that empower your team and provide clear direction will help to improve your team's performance, increase productivity, and cultivate a higher degree of innovation.

Effective decision-making ensures that technology is implemented strategically, is aligned with organizational goals, and is adopted smoothly by the team and stakeholders.

The ability to make sound decisions under pressure, considering various risks and potential outcomes, enables you to navigate challenges, adapt to changing circumstances, and protect the organization's interests.

Technical leaders who consistently make effective decisions earn a reputation for strategic thinking, sound judgment, and the ability to guide the organization towards success.

When team members witness effective decision-making, they gain confidence in their leader's abilities and are inspired to contribute their best efforts to the organization's success.

In the ever-changing world of technology, effective decision-making is not just a skill; it is a compass that guides technical leaders through the complexities of their roles. By gathering comprehensive information, considering diverse perspectives, and aligning decisions with strategic goals, you can make informed judgments that drive innovation, empower your team, and shape the future of technology.

Section 4: Shaping the Future of Technology

Welcome to the exciting world of shaping the future of technology! In this section, you'll dive into the latest trends that are revolutionizing the tech landscape, learning how to position yourself and your team at the forefront of innovation.

Get ready to become an expert at identifying and evaluating emerging technologies, assessing their potential impact, and developing strategies to integrate them into your organization's operations. You'll also discover how to create a culture of innovation within your team, encouraging creativity, and empowering your team members to take risks and pursue new ideas.

By understanding the forces shaping the future of technology and developing the skills to navigate them, you can become a leader who not only adapts to change but also drives it. This section will provide you with the knowledge and tools you need to play a pivotal role in shaping the future of technology and making a lasting impact on the world. So, grab your thinking cap and get ready to embark on this journey to becoming a tech leader of the future!

Innovation: Leading the Charge for Technological Advancement

Innovation is the lifeblood of progress, and technical leaders play a pivotal role in driving technological advancements and shaping the future. Innovation is not just about inventing new technologies; it is about identifying opportunities, challenging assumptions, and transforming ideas into reality. Technical leaders who embrace innovation can inspire their teams, lead the charge for technological advancement, and position their organizations at the forefront of progress.

The Essence of Innovation in Technical Leadership

Innovation is not a random act; it is a deliberate and structured process that requires a blend of creativity, critical thinking, and a passion for solving problems.

By fostering a culture of innovation you will encourage creativity, risk-taking, and experimentation within your team, creating an environment where new ideas are welcomed and explored.

Actively seek out opportunities for innovation, identifying challenges and unmet needs that can be addressed through new technologies or approaches.

Encourage your team to question assumptions, challenge the status quo, and explore unconventional solutions.

View setbacks and failures as opportunities for learning and growth, fostering a resilience that allows your team to persevere and refine their ideas.

Fostering collaboration and cross-functional thinking will encourage your team members to draw upon diverse perspectives and expertise to drive innovation.

Strategies for Fostering Innovation in Technical Teams

Cultivating innovation in technical teams requires that you take a strategic approach that addresses both individual and team dynamics.

To encourage innovation, you need to paint a clear picture of what you want to achieve and break it down into actionable steps. Think of it like planning a road trip. You need a destination (vision) and a set of directions (goals) to get there. With a clear roadmap, your team can navigate the innovation landscape with confidence, reaching new heights of creativity and success.

Create a space where ideas can flow freely. Encourage your team to share their perspectives, no matter how unconventional. Let ideas spark and ignite, leading to new possibilities.

Provide your team with the tools and resources they need to make their ideas a reality. Allocate funding, training, and access to the latest technologies. With these resources at their disposal, your team can transform their innovative ideas into tangible solutions.

When your team achieves innovative breakthroughs, don't forget to celebrate their success. Recognize their efforts, highlight their achievements, and make sure their accomplishments are known throughout the organization. Encourage them to share their learnings and best practices, spreading the innovation magic within the team.

Encourage a growth mindset within the team, emphasizing the importance of continuous learning, adaptability, and resilience in the face of challenges.

Value and encourage diversity of thought and perspectives, recognizing that different experiences and backgrounds can lead to innovative solutions.

Encourage experimentation and calculated risk-taking, providing a safe space for team members to explore new ideas and approaches without fear of reprisal.

To ensure your innovative solutions hit the mark, establish feedback loops that gather insights from stakeholders and users. This continuous feedback mechanism will help you identify areas for improvement and refine your solutions, ensuring they truly meet the needs of those they are designed for.

The Impact of Innovation on Technical Leadership

Innovation is the driving force behind technological advancement and organizational success.

To truly lead the pack, establish your organization as a beacon of innovation and progress in your industry. Attract the best and brightest minds by showcasing your commitment to innovation and shaping the future of technology. With a reputation for groundbreaking ideas and a knack for solving real-world problems, your organization will stand out as a leader, attracting top talent and leaving a lasting impact on the world.

To stay ahead of the curve, continuously innovate and develop products, services, and processes that set your organization apart from the competition. These innovative solutions will not only give your organization a competitive edge but also solidify its position as a leader in the market. With a constant stream of groundbreaking ideas, your organization will remain at the forefront, leaving competitors in its wake.

Use your innovative prowess to tackle real-world problems and make a positive impact on society. Develop solutions that address critical societal challenges and enhance the lives of others. With a focus on improving well-being and creating a better world, your organization can make a meaningful difference and leave a lasting legacy.

To attract and retain the best and brightest minds, cultivate a work environment that's a magnet for innovation and creativity. Create a space where talented individuals feel valued, empowered, and excited to contribute their unique perspectives. Let them know that their ideas are cherished, their growth is nurtured, and their contributions make a real difference. With a culture that fosters innovation and embraces diverse perspectives, your organization will become a haven for top talent, attracting and retaining the individuals who will shape the future.

Innovation is not a luxury in the ever-evolving world of technology; it is an essential ingredient for survival and success. Technical leaders who embrace innovation, empower their teams, and lead the charge for technological advancement are the architects of the future. By fostering a culture of creativity, challenging assumptions, and transforming ideas into reality, you can position your organization at the forefront of progress.

Strategic Vision: Guiding Your Organization Towards Technological Success

In the ever-changing tech landscape, where innovation is king and adaptation is the key to survival, effective technical leadership demands a clear and inspiring vision. This vision serves as the road map, guiding the organization's technological journey and shaping its future. Technical leaders with the power to articulate this vision become the driving force behind their teams, uniting stakeholders, and positioning their organizations to thrive in the ever-evolving tech world.

Strategic vision isn't just about daydreaming or predicting the future; it's about understanding where your organization stands now, identifying potential breakthroughs, and mapping a path to achieving long-term goals. Effective technical leaders with a strategic vision are the architects of their organization's technological future.

You need a deep grasp of your organization's overall goals, strategic objectives, and the challenges you face in the competitive tech arena. You're like a cartographer, mapping out the organization's position and the obstacles it must overcome.

As a keen observer of the technological landscape, you should be constantly scanning for emerging trends, disruptive technologies, and potential shifts that could impact your organization's future. You are the early-bird explorer, scouting for new paths and opportunities.

You seamlessly integrate technological advancements with the organization's overall strategy, ensuring that technology isn't just a tool but a driving force for innovation, growth, and competitive advantage.

When it comes to communication, you need to be a master storyteller, weaving the strategic vision into a clear, concise, and inspiring narrative. Your words ignite a fire within team members, stakeholders, and the organization as a whole, rallying everyone behind the shared vision.

You also need to understand that the technological landscape is ever-changing like a river constantly flowing. You should be adaptable, a flexible thinker, ready to adapt and refine the strategic vision as needed to stay relevant, embrace emerging opportunities, and navigate challenges

Strategies for Formulating and Articulating a Strategic Vision

As a technical leader, shaping and articulating a strategic vision is not a one-person job; it's a collaborative journey that requires careful consideration and diverse perspectives. To effectively develop and communicate your strategic vision, embrace these effective strategies:

Delve into a thorough analysis of your organization's current position, the competitive landscape it navigates, emerging technological trends, and the potential opportunities and challenges that lie ahead.

Gather valuable insights, perspectives, and potential areas of focus by engaging with key stakeholders, including executives, team members, industry experts, and potential customers. Their diverse viewpoints will enrich your vision.

Articulate the core components of your strategic vision with clarity and precision. Clearly outline the organization's desired future state, the role of technology in achieving that state, and the key milestones and objectives that will guide the journey.

Weave the strategic vision into a captivating narrative that resonates with your audience. Ensure the narrative is easy to understand, inspiring, and aligns with the organization's values and aspirations.

Communicate the strategic vision to all stakeholders, utilizing a variety of channels such as presentations, town halls, and one-on-one conversations. Ensure that everyone is aligned, understands their role in achieving the vision, and feels empowered to contribute.

The Impact of Strategic Vision on Technical Leadership

A well-articulated and effectively communicated strategic vision has a profound impact on the success of technical leaders and the organizations they serve.

Embrace a shared strategic vision, and you'll align your team members, providing them with direction, purpose, and the empowerment to contribute their expertise towards achieving common goals. With a shared vision, your team members become united in their efforts, working together seamlessly to achieve the organization's objectives.

Adopt a strategic vision as your guiding framework, and you'll make informed decisions about technology investments, resource allocation, and strategic initiatives. With a clear vision to guide you, you'll make strategic choices that align with the organization's overall goals and propel it towards a successful future.

Articulate a clear strategic vision, and you'll secure buy-in and support from stakeholders, including executives, investors, and customers. By clearly communicating your vision, you'll foster a collaborative environment where everyone understands the organization's direction and is invested in its success. This collaboration will spark innovation and growth, propelling the organization forward.

Craft a compelling strategic vision, and you'll attract and retain top talent. Individuals who seek opportunities to contribute to meaningful change and make a positive impact in the technological landscape will be drawn to your organization. With a strong vision, you'll build a team of talented individuals who are passionate about driving innovation and making a lasting impact.

Establish a strategic vision, and you'll position your organization for long-term success. With a clear vision as your compass, you'll be able to navigate the ever-changing technological landscape, adapt to emerging trends, and seize new opportunities. Your organization will be well-equipped to thrive in the dynamic tech world, securing its success for years to come.

In the world of technology, the pace of change is relentless and uncertainty is the norm. Effective technical leadership hinges on a clear and compelling strategic vision. Technical leaders who can articulate a strategic vision, inspire others to embrace it, and adapt it as needed are not just guiding their organizations towards technological success; they are shaping the future of technology itself. By embracing strategic foresight, you can become a catalyst for innovation, empower your team to make a lasting impact and leave an indelible mark on the technological landscape.

Effective Delegation: Leveraging the Power of Your Team

In a dynamic sector, technical leaders face a constant demand for their time and expertise. However, the ability to effectively delegate tasks and responsibilities is not a sign of weakness but rather a mark of effective leadership. By delegating, you can empower your teams, leverage the collective talents of their members, and focus on higher-level strategic initiatives.

The Essence of Effective Delegation for Technical Leaders

Effective delegation is not about simply handing off tasks; it is about creating an environment where team members feel trusted, equipped, and empowered to contribute their best efforts. To delegate effectively, consider the following keys.

Understand your team members' strengths and skills. This will enable you to delegate tasks that align with individual capabilities.

Provide clear expectations, goals, and deadlines for delegated tasks, ensuring that team members understand their responsibilities and have the necessary context to succeed.

Empower your team members to make informed decisions within their scope of authority, fostering a sense of ownership and accountability.

Provide ongoing support and guidance, ensuring that team members have access to the resources and information they need to complete their tasks successfully.

Recognize and reward your team members' individual contributions. This demonstrates your appreciation for their efforts and reinforces the value of delegation.

Strategies for Effective Delegation in Technical Teams

Delegation requires a thoughtful and strategic approach. Evaluate each task's complexity, required skills, and potential impact to determine the most suitable team member to delegate it to.

Then, clearly articulate the task's objectives, deliverables, expectations, and any relevant background information or context the assigned team member will need to complete the task.

Set clear milestones and schedule regular check-ins to monitor progress, provide feedback, and address any challenges promptly.

Foster open communication, encouraging team members to ask questions, raise concerns, and seek clarification whenever needed.

Delegate tasks that provide opportunities for your team members to expand their skills, to gain new experiences, and contribute to their professional development.

The Impact of Effective Delegation on Technical Leadership

Effective delegation has a significant impact on the success of technical leaders and the organizations they serve.

Delegation empowers team members, increases engagement, and fosters a sense of ownership and responsibility, leading to improved performance and productivity.

Effective delegation allows you, as a technical leader, to focus on higher-level strategic initiatives, improve overall team capacity, and optimize resource utilization.

Delegation encourages diverse perspectives, collaboration, and cross-functional problem-solving, leading to enhanced innovation and more effective solutions.

Delegation provides opportunities for your team members to develop their skills, gain experience, and prepare for future leadership roles, contributing to talent development and succession planning.

Effective delegation leads to increased job satisfaction, reduces burnout, and improves retention rates, as team members feel valued, trusted, and empowered to contribute their expertise.

In the complex and ever-evolving world of technology, effective delegation is not just a skill; it is a cornerstone of successful technical leadership. By mastering the art of delegation, you can unleash the collective potential of your teams, drive innovation, and position your organization for long-term success. By empowering your team members, providing opportunities for growth, and fostering a culture of trust and collaboration, you can transform your teams into engines of innovation and propel your organization to new heights in the ever-changing technological landscape.

Influencing without Authority: Building Trust and Respect

Technical leadership often extends beyond formal titles and hierarchical positions. Effective leadership is not solely about wielding authority but also about the ability to influence others through genuine trust, respect, and a shared vision for success. Technical leaders who can influence without authority are able to inspire, motivate, and guide their teams towards achieving common goals, even without the power of formal authority.

The Essence of Influencing without Authority for Technical Leaders

Influencing without authority is not about manipulating or coercing others; it is about building meaningful relationships, earning respect through expertise and integrity, and fostering a collaborative environment where team members feel valued and empowered to contribute their best efforts.

Build credibility by demonstrating your technical competence, sharing your knowledge generously, and consistently delivering valuable results.

Actively listen to your team members' perspectives, understand their concerns, and empathize with their challenges, creating a supportive and inclusive environment.

Communicate your ideas clearly, concisely, and persuasively, tailoring your communication style to suit different audiences and fostering a shared understanding of goals and objectives.

Lead by example. Set the standard for behaviour, inspiring others to follow your lead through your actions and commitment to excellence.

Empower team members to take ownership of their work, by providing guidance and support without stifling individual creativity and problem-solving abilities.

Strategies for Influencing without Authority in Technical Teams

Building trust and respect, and influencing others without authority, requires a consistent and genuine approach. To influence your team members without relying on formal authority, cultivate strong relationships with your team members, get to know them as individuals, understand their motivations, and value their unique perspectives.

Approach situations with humility, acknowledging your own limitations, and being open to learning from others' experiences and insights.

Regularly recognize and appreciate team members' contributions, both big and small, fostering a sense of value and reinforcing positive behaviour.

Foster a culture of collaboration and shared ownership, encouraging team members to work together, share ideas, and contribute to collective success.

Encourage team members to pursue continuous learning and growth, providing opportunities for skill development, knowledge sharing, and professional advancement.

The Impact of Influencing without Authority on Technical Leadership

Influencing without authority has a profound impact on the effectiveness of technical leaders and the organizations they serve.

It results in increased team cohesion and morale. Building trust and respect leads to increased motivation, engagement, and collective effort.

A collaborative environment fueled by mutual respect encourages knowledge sharing, cross-functional collaboration, and a willingness to experiment with new ideas, leading to enhanced innovation.

Team members' willingness to share ideas, challenge assumptions, and contribute diverse perspectives leads to more effective problem-solving and informed decision-making.

A team built on trust and respect is better equipped to adapt to change, navigate challenges, and bounce back from setbacks.

Developing a reputation for influencing without authority attracts and retains top talent, individuals who seek opportunities to work in a supportive, collaborative, and empowering environment.

Effective technical leadership extends beyond formal authority. Technical leaders who can influence without authority, by building trust, fostering respect, and empowering their teams, are not just leading their teams; they are shaping the future of technology. By embracing influence as a leadership tool, you can inspire your team to achieve remarkable results, drive transformative change, and leave a lasting impact on the technological landscape.

Part 5: The Personal Transformation of a Technical Leader

In this final section, we'll delve into the personal growth and development required to excel as a tech leader. We'll explore the importance of self-awareness, feedback, work-life balance, and building a lasting legacy.

As you progress through this section, you'll discover strategies to enhance your self-awareness, embrace feedback as a valuable tool for growth, cultivate a healthy work-life balance, and leave a lasting impact on the world of technology. These personal transformations will empower you to lead with greater effectiveness, inspire your team, and make a significant contribution to the ever-evolving landscape of technology.

Whether you're an aspiring tech leader or a seasoned professional seeking to elevate your leadership, this section will provide you with the insights and guidance you need to become a truly exceptional tech leader.

Developing Self-Awareness: The Key to Continuous Improvement

Self-awareness is the cornerstone of effective leadership. Technical leaders who possess a deep understanding of their own strengths, weaknesses, biases, and motivations are better equipped to make informed decisions, navigate complex situations, and lead their teams towards success. Self-awareness is not a static trait; it is an ongoing journey of self-discovery, reflection, and personal growth.

The Essence of Self-Awareness for Technical Leaders

Self-awareness is not about being perfect or having all the answers; it is about understanding your own limitations, identifying areas for improvement, and actively seeking feedback to refine your leadership skills.

Recognizing your own strengths and weaknesses will provide you with a clear understanding of the areas where they excel, and the areas where you need to develop further.

Being aware of your own biases and assumptions, you are able to actively work to mitigate their impact on your decisions and interactions.

Actively seeking feedback from others, both positive and negative, will allow you to regularly reflect on your experiences to identify areas for growth.

Always be open to learning new things, expanding your knowledge base, and refining your skills throughout your career.

Maintaining a high level of emotional intelligence, enables you to understand your own emotions, manage your reactions effectively, and empathize with others.

Strategies for Developing Self-Awareness as a Technical Leader

Enhancing self-awareness requires a commitment to personal growth and a willingness to engage in introspection.

Seek feedback from multiple sources. Regularly solicit feedback from colleagues, supervisors, mentors, and direct reports, gaining diverse perspectives on your leadership strengths and areas for improvement.

Keep a journal or reflective log. Use it to document your experiences, reflect on your actions and decisions, and identify patterns or recurring themes.

Utilise self-assessment tools, such as personality tests or 360-degree feedback surveys, to gain insights into your strengths, weaknesses, and leadership style.

Seek mentorship and guidance from experienced leaders who can provide valuable insights, coaching, and support on your journey of self-discovery.

Practice mindfulness and emotional intelligence. Engage in mindfulness practices, such as meditation or journaling, to enhance self-awareness, manage emotions effectively, and cultivate empathy.

The Impact of Self-Awareness on Technical Leadership

Self-awareness has a profound impact on the effectiveness of technical leaders and the organizations they serve. As a self-aware leader, you are be able to make more informed decisions, considering your own biases, limitations, and the perspectives of others.

With enhanced emotional Intelligence you can communicate more effectively, empathise with team members, manage conflict constructively, and foster a positive work environment.

Being self-aware increases your adaptability and resilience. You are better equipped to adapt to change, navigate challenges, and learn from setbacks, contributing to team resilience and long-term success.

Demonstrating self-awareness builds stronger relationships with your team members, fostering trust, respect, and a sense of shared purpose.

With a commitment to personal growth, you are continuously seeking opportunities to refine your skills, expand your knowledge, and become a more effective leader.

Self-awareness is not just a desirable trait for technical leaders; it is an essential ingredient for success. Technical leaders who cultivate self-awareness, embrace continuous learning, and lead with authenticity and empathy are not just guiding their teams towards technological advancements; they are shaping the future of technology itself. By embarking on a journey of self-discovery and actively seeking ways to improve, you can become a catalyst for positive change, inspiring your team to achieve remarkable results and leave a lasting impact on the technological landscape.

Embracing Feedback: Learning from Mistakes and Successes

Feedback is a crucial tool for growth and improvement in any field. It provides valuable insights into our strengths and weaknesses, our successes and failures, and helps us identify areas where we can refine our skills and enhance our leadership effectiveness. Technical leaders who can effectively seek, receive, and apply feedback are better equipped to navigate the complexities of the technological landscape, make informed decisions, and guide their teams towards achieving common goals.

The Essence of Embracing Feedback for Technical Leaders

Embracing feedback is not about being perfect or infallible; it is about recognizing that we can always learn and grow from the experiences and perspectives of others.

Actively seek feedback from colleagues, mentors, stakeholders, and even those who may have differing perspectives or opinions, recognizing the value of diverse viewpoints.

Create a culture of open communication and psychological safety, encouraging team members to share their honest opinions and concerns without fear of judgment or repercussions.

Understand the difference between constructive feedback and personal criticism. And then focus on the valuable insights gained from feedback while letting go of unproductive negativity.

Objectively analyze feedback, considering its relevance, validity, and potential impact on your leadership approach and decision-making.

Develop an action plan for improvement. The plan should address the areas you have identified for growth, incorporating feedback into your personal and professional development goals.

Strategies for Effectively Seeking and Receiving Feedback

Effectively seeking and receiving feedback requires a proactive and receptive approach. Following are some strategies to enhance your ability to gather and utilize feedback as a technical leader.

Create regular feedback mechanisms, such as one-on-one meetings, team retrospectives, or anonymous feedback surveys, to gather input from colleagues and team members.

Foster a culture of open and honest communication, encouraging team members to feel comfortable sharing their perspectives, concerns, and suggestions without fear of reprisal.

Ask specific questions to elicit valuable insights, such as "What are some areas where I can improve my leadership style?" or "How could I have handled that situation differently?"

Practice active listening, giving your full attention to the feedback provider, demonstrating empathy, and seeking to understand their perspective.

Acknowledge the feedback, express gratitude for their input, and assure them that their insights will be considered and addressed.

The Impact of Embracing Feedback on Technical Leadership

Embracing feedback has a profound impact on your success as a technical leader and the organization you serve.

Feedback provides valuable insights into different perspectives, potential risks, and alternative approaches, leading to more informed decision-making and effective problem-solving.

Feedback serves as a catalyst for continuous improvement, enabling you to identify areas for development, expand your skillset, and enhance your leadership effectiveness.

Embracing feedback fosters trust and strengthens relationships within the team, creating a supportive environment where individuals feel valued and heard.

The ability to learn from feedback equips you to adapt to change, navigate challenges, and bounce back from setbacks.

Feedback from team members encourages shared ownership, empowers individuals to contribute their perspectives, and fosters a collaborative approach to problem-solving.

In the ever-changing world of technology, embracing feedback is not just a skill; it is a defining characteristic of successful technical leadership. Technical leaders who approach feedback with openness, humility, and a growth mindset are not just shaping the future of technology; they are shaping the future of themselves, their teams, and the organizations they have the privilege of leading. By embracing feedback as a valuable tool for growth and improvement, you can become a catalyst for positive change, empower your team to achieve remarkable results, and leave a lasting impact on the technological landscape.

Maintaining a Healthy Work-Life Balance: Nurturing Your Well-being

In a fast-paced and demanding industry, finding a balance between your professional life and your personal well-being is crucial for technical leaders to thrive. It's not about achieving a perfect 50/50 split; it's about finding a rhythm that works for you, allowing you to excel in your career while also having time for the things that matter most to you outside of work.

The Balancing Act for Technical Leaders

A healthy work-life balance isn't just about having more time for leisure activities and personal pursuits. It's about ensuring that you're not constantly burning the midnight oil, feeling overwhelmed and stressed, and eventually crashing and burning. It's about making sure that you're taking care of your physical and mental health, so you can show up as your best self for your team, your family, and yourself.

To master the art of work-life balance you need to establish clear boundaries between work and personal time, prioritizing tasks and commitments to avoid burnout and ensure adequate time for personal pursuits.

Leverage technology tools to streamline work processes, automate tasks, and improve productivity, freeing up time for personal pursuits.

You need to trust your team and empower them to take ownership, reducing your workload and allowing you to focus on strategic initiatives and personal well-being.

Prioritize self-care practices, such as regular exercise, healthy eating habits, and mindfulness techniques, to maintain your physical and mental health.

It is important that you schedule regular breaks throughout the workday and disconnect from work during non-work hours to allow for mental rejuvenation and personal time. Schedule personal time like it's a work meeting. Block out time in your calendar for personal activities, hobbies, and social interactions, ensuring that they are not overshadowed by work commitments.

Clearly communicate your work hours, availability, and boundaries to colleagues and clients, setting expectations for communication and response times.

Encourage and support a company culture that values work-life balance, offering flexible work arrangements, wellness programs, and recognition for personal achievements.

Recognize when to seek support from colleagues, mentors, or professional resources to address work-related stress or personal challenges. Seek guidance from mentors or experienced leaders who have successfully navigated work-life balance, gaining insights and strategies for maintaining a healthy equilibrium.

The Positive Impact of Work-Life Balance on Technical Leadership

A healthy work-life balance has a profound impact on the success of technical leaders and the organizations they serve.

As a leader who prioritizes their well-being you are more present, engaged, and effective in your leadership role, making informed decisions and inspiring your team.

A balanced lifestyle reduces stress, promotes creativity, and enhances problem-solving abilities, leading to increased productivity and innovation.

Prioritizing your personal well-being prevents burnout, promotes mental health, and fosters a positive mindset, contributing to a more fulfilling and sustainable leadership journey.

Fostering a culture of work-life balance promotes employee satisfaction, reduces turnover, and creates a more engaged and motivated workforce.

Prioritizing your well-being makes you better equipped to handle challenges, navigate change, and adapt to the ever-evolving technological landscape.

In the demanding world of technology, achieving work-life balance is not a luxury; it is a necessity for effective leadership. Technical leaders who prioritize their well-being, nurture healthy boundaries, and empower their teams are not just shaping the future of technology; they are shaping the future of themselves, their families, and the organizations they have the privilege of leading.

Leaving a Lasting Legacy: The Impact of a Technical Leader

In the fast-paced and ever-changing world of tech, you're not just a manager or a problem-solver; you're a potential legacy-builder. Technical leaders have the power to shape the future, inspire generations, and leave a lasting mark on the world we live in.

But leaving a legacy isn't about getting your name in the headlines or amassing a fortune; it's about making a real and meaningful impact on the world through technology. It's about creating something that will outlast your time, something that will inspire others to follow in your footsteps.

The Making of a Technical Legacy

Leaving a lasting legacy isn't about being perfect or having all the answers; it's about being willing to learn, grow, and make a difference.

Technical leaders who leave a lasting legacy don't just follow the status quo; they push the boundaries of what's possible. They create a culture of innovation where creativity and experimentation are encouraged, leading to groundbreaking advancements that shape the future of tech.

Recognize that the real power of tech lies in the people who use it. Invest in your team members, nurturing their skills, empowering them to contribute their unique talents, and creating a collective force for innovation.

Never stop learning. Don't be afraid to admit you don't know everything. Embrace a growth mindset, constantly seeking new knowledge, expanding your horizons, and encouraging others to do the same. Your commitment to learning fuels innovation and keeps your team at the forefront of tech.

Don't just chase the next big thing; consider the impact of your decisions. Uphold the highest ethical standards, ensuring that technological advancements align with societal values and responsible practices. Your leadership sets the tone for a positive impact on your team and organisation.

More than leading your team; mentor and inspire future leaders. Share your knowledge, experiences, and passion for tech with others. Doing this will ignite a spark in the next generation of innovators and leaders, ensuring the continued advancement of technology.

Leadership isn't just about managing teams, solving problems, or achieving short-term goals. It's about leaving a lasting legacy, shaping the future of technology, and inspiring generations to come. Tech leaders who embrace this responsibility, lead with vision, empower their teams, and champion innovation have the power to transform their organisations for the better.

FROM DEVELOPER TO TECH LEAD

Elevate Your Skills, Empower Your Team, and Shape the Future

As you embark on your journey from Developer to Tech Lead, this comprehensive guide will equip you with the knowledge, skills, and mindset to excel in your role.
Chart your own journey to technical leadership, gaining insights into the essential skills and qualities that set exceptional leaders apart.
Develop strategies for deepening your technical expertise, cultivating a growth mindset, and becoming a tech trendspotter.
Master the art of empowering teams, fostering a collaborative environment through effective conflict resolution, and making sound decisions under pressure.

ABOUT THE AUTHOR

Owen is a self-taught developer with a tech career spanning more than 20 years. Having started as a novice designer he is currently heading a large team of developers in one of Ireland's premiere e-commerce agencies.